RONDEAU REVUE

Edited by

Andrew Head

First published in Great Britain in 1998 by
POETRY NOW
1-2 Wainman Road, Woodston,
Peterborough, PE2 7BU
Telephone (01733) 230746
Fax (01733) 230751

All Rights Reserved

Copyright Contributors 1998

HB ISBN 1 86188 656 X
SB ISBN 1 86188 651 9

FOREWORD

Although we are a nation of poetry writers we are accused of not reading poetry and not buying poetry books: after many years of listening to the incessant gripes of poetry publishers, I can only assume that the books they publish, in general, are books that most people do not want to read.

Poetry should not be obscure, introverted, and as cryptic as a crossword puzzle: it is the poet's duty to reach out and embrace the world.

The world owes the poet nothing and we should not be expected to dig and delve into a rambling discourse searching for some inner meaning.

The reason we write poetry (and almost all of us do) is because we want to communicate: an ideal; an idea; or a specific feeling. Poetry is as essential in communication, as a letter; a radio; a telephone, and the main criteria for selecting the poems in this anthology is very simple: they communicate.

Poetry is an open and universal art-form; as with other creative forms, it has many aspects and can be appreciated on different levels. Poetry's boundaries are as free and wide-ranging as the language from which it is composed. It is only by constantly expanding the boundaries that any art can grow.

All written in the traditional form of the Rondeau, the poetry in this anthology is diverse in subject matter and the poets have written from the heart. Poetry is a window to the soul, a pursuit through which we can understand more of ourselves.

Contents

Let's Go To War	Jean Paisley	1
They Thought It Right	Margaret Connor	2
Which Way?	John Richard Sergeant	3
Keys	Mary Payne	4
The Virtuous Assassin	Margret Shaw	5
A Tiny Quiver	Ann Richardson	6
My Father's Face	Edward McErlane	7
Rondel - Gloria	John Widdows	8
The Bottle Beckons	Jan Whitfield	9
My Heart Is Heavy	Joan Scher	10
From The Abandoned	Emma Walkers	11
Pure Gold	Barbara Henry	12
Listen -The Wind	Eve Webber	13
Rescue Dog	Bee Kenchington	14
Magic Moments	Sylvia R Reader	15
All My Heart	Hilary Philips	16
I Try To Control	Colin Farmer	17
Nature	Richard Saunders	18
I'm Older Now	Angela Helen	19
When Darkness Falls	George Stanworth	20
That Dream	Peter Chaney	21
He Was My Son	Karen Tyas	22
My First Rondeau	Peggy Johnson	23
Bell Echoes	Shirley Beckett	24
Life's Garden	Joyce Goldie	25
Princess	Elizabeth Rice	26
The Ghost	Ann Mather	27
Tropical Rains	Jan Claxton	28
This Is The City	Harry Livesey	29
My Labrador	John Christopher	30
I Do Think On	Julie Brace	31
Time To Sleep	A B Chabaluk	32
I'm Taking It Back!	Verleta Malcolm	33
Needs	Pat Eves	34
The Mirror	Marian Acres	35
Anne	Suzan Gumush	36

The Tide Has Turned	Dorothy E Richardson	37
Up Signal Hill	Mary E Cowburn	38
This Garden	Jay	39
In The Garden	J A A Sharp	40
Radiant Moon	Gueta Craigie	41
Back Home	Betty Curnow	42
Total Security	Peter Vaughan Williams	43
On The Pavement	Shirley Johnson	44
The Promises Of Love	Jean Marsden	45
The Tick Has Stopped	Katherine Jane Rawlings	46
A Game	Margaret D'Sa	47
The Tornado	Elizabeth Melvin	48
The Month Of May	Heather Middleton	49
I'm Glad I'm Not	Roger Williams	50
A Lovely Smile	Brenda Thorne	51
Meandering Down	Mark Boardman	52
Urban Daydream	Shirley Richmond	53
Again	F McFaul	54
So Long Ago . . .	Richard Styles	55
Rondeau For The First Day Of Spring	Andrew Fisher	56
Love's Rondeau	Barbara Stanworth	57
Plight Of The Few	M C Davies	58
Fishermen	Eric McClurry	59
Those Childhood Dreams	Sylvia Crocker	60
I'm Alone	Patricia-Mary Gross	61
Ought For A Laff	J H Watson	62
I Close My Eyes	Jo Spencer	63
This Was 1997	Petina Anderson	64
He's Better Off	Barbara Knight	65
Older And Wiser	Terry Edwards	66
Old Truant Boys' Reunion	Ian MacLaren	67
Searching	C J Collins-Reed	68
Ode To A Tiger	Betty Green	69
Almost Winter	S H Smith	70
I Am Not Young	Katrina M Greenhalf	71
They'll Never Know	Christine Nicholson	72
Theodore	Judith Stinton	73

Sailing	Barbara Pearton	74
Of Love	Paul Corrigan	75
Fine Wines	Pat Derbyshire	76
When You Want Me	DJ King	77
A Way Out Fishy Tale	Rosemary Keith	78
I Fall Asleep	John Aldred	79
Just Fishing	Pauline Pullan	80
The Two Happy Ones	John Amsden	81
Spring Treads Softly	Ivy Allpress	82
No Recipe	Mary Anne Scott	83
Our Poor Earth	J D Bailey	84
I Give Up	J C Fearnley	85
Think Of The Words	Albert Moses	86
Trust Me He Said	Hazel Wilson	87
I Never Learn	Peter Madle	88
Grannie's Little Angels	Patricia Cairns Laird	89
Out Of The Darkness	Shelia Scott	90
Millennium Rondeau	Kath Hurley	91
Glass Shards Shattered And Splintered	Kathrine Talbot	92
Soaps	M E Lavin	93
Now	Jack Greaves	94
Winter's Gift	Gwen Stone	95
No More Goodbyes!	Eleanor Rogers	96
Stranger	Guy Fletcher	97
Love Is Caring	W Beavill	98
Follow The Sun	Jan Ingram McCaffery	99
Time Stands Still	Anne Jones	100
I Will Try Again	Mildred Mayes	101
I Love My Garden	Lisa Wolfe	102
I Shall Not Cry	Margaret Winrow	103
Do Eat These Nuts	Nicholas Winn	104
Flip	Aidan Baker	105
Bathed In The Moonlight	Jack Judd	106
Evacuation	Doreen Welby	107
Hold On	Pamela Girdlestone	108

LET'S GO TO WAR

Serve up those few ideas let's go to war
We've tried them all before,
They tore our minds to pieces shredded
conscience to the core,
strip off the shorts and football shirts galore,
who wants to drink with friends and count the score.

Those pop records that kept us from our sleep,
we'll burn the lot there's none we wish to keep,
until the clubs have emptied one by one,
our parents might not know that we have gone,
who wants to marry and take on a wife,
to fill the world with one more extra life,
serve up those few ideas let's go to war.

Those holidays abroad with friends in Spain,
we'll think of balmy Britain in the rain,
for King and Country we can stand up proud,
as for our parents they can buy the shroud,
what's man without ideas even raw
serve up those few ideas let's go to war.

Jean Paisley

THEY THOUGHT IT RIGHT

She thought it right to lead him on
then let him dangle - nothing won -
nor did she bargain that he might
end up in a pathetic plight,

and only after he had gone,
she idly wondered what she'd done
to cause him pain and make him run.
Was she a witch with second sight?

She thought it right
to test her powers and have some fun
and couldn't have foreseen that gun
or those black moments in the night.
Oh no, she never guessed her light
would fail her with the setting sun -
he thought it right.

Margaret Connor

WHICH WAY?

Which way did they go I wonder
Which way did they go?
The Welshman with his dog called Ronda
Which way did they go?

Did they go to the park up yonder
To let old Ronda bark and wander
And did they then return to town
To rest and Ronda to lay down
Which way did they go?

At last at last the secret's out
We have had a fall of snow
So now I have no need to ponder
I followed their footprints
Way up yonder
So thanks to all that snow
I really really know
Which way they did go.

John Richard Sergeant

KEYS

The bunch of keys that know no doors
Lie jumbled in the cluttered drawers;
I clear them out, my job is done,
A life is finished, I go on.

Looking around at rooms so bare,
Remembering times when love dwelt there,
I pack the past into its place,
Until then my fingers slowly trace
The bunch of keys.

I felt your presence, somehow knew
I'd found the final link to you.
To lock up treasured memories,
My answer was to cherish these:
The bunch of keys.

Mary Payne

THE VIRTUOUS ASSASSIN

'Not for oneself but for others'. Her school
maxim. 'Non sibi sed alia'. A rule
to guide girls of virtue, selfless pledge,
that led inexorably to this ledge.

Selfless - less - gone. Duty, obdurate mule,
held fast. The dark pearl deeps said 'Come,' said 'Fool,'
sed alia. Offer'd oblivion. Yet, judge
not for oneself.

Self, denied, died. Left a threadbare spool.
And now, beside her shopping bag, a pool
forms. She sighs, and, reluctant, leaves the bridge.
Goes to preserve fish fingers in the fridge.
Now, e'en small concerns, her own desires cool.
Not for oneself.

Margret Shaw

A Tiny Quiver

A tiny quiver of her lips,
A tear brushed off with finger tips.
She's leaving love for world of fear,
To him she goes, where all she'll hear
Is sit down, get out, booze he sips.

Each day drags on, no longed for trips,
He stands there looming, hands on hips,
Below him, precious, gentle, near,
      A tiny quiver on her lips.

Then Friday comes, in drunken fits,
He bangs the wall, beside him sits
My little love, so fair, so dear,
Smiling now, 'cause grandma's here
      A tiny quiver on her lips.

Ann Richardson

My Father's Face

Today I saw my father's face
A jewel set in a wooden case
Of life bereft and marble cold
His folded tallow hand I hold
In casket lined in purple lace
I stand his guard with staff and mace
This tollund man no longer old
I saw my father's face

The salty sting of death I taste
A rosary of tears I trace
As down my cheeks so shall they roll
And fall away through every fold
No man can ever take his place
I saw my father's face.

Edward McErlane

Rondel - Gloria

Father, to Thee at dawn be praise
And glory to the Holy Three,
The Trinity in Unity.

And in the zenith of our days
To the Son also worship be.
Father, to Thee at dawn be praise
And glory to the Holy Three.

Then, in the night, with prayer we raise
To Paraclete our psalmody,
Love's advocate in charity.
Father, to Thee at dawn be praise
And glory to the Holy Three,
The Trinity in Unity.

John Widdows

The Bottle Beckons

The bottle beckons, gleaming amber bright
Just one small measure will help her sleep tonight
And in her cup she pours a generous gill,
a little more to ward off winter's chill,
She says. And knows that she is right.

And on the morning after, a pick-me-up just might
Assuage the pounding temples where duelling demons fight
One swift embrace will bid them all be still
The bottle beckons.

An old and friendly Dracula with warm familiar bite
whose tantalising twisted smile continue to invite
A sympathetic Satan, he does not control her will
No master, but a servant whom she commands - until
with double-dealing promise of troubles put to flight
The bottle beckons.

Jan Whitfield

MY HEART IS HEAVY

My heart is heavy, but I do not cry,
As my mind wanders, through years gone by.
And I look at my grandchildren, how they grow,
Entering a life they do not know.
What is to come, where will they go?

I dare not go out in the streets at night.
Each soul in the dark, fills me with such fright.
I thank the Lord, I don't live alone . . .
My heart is heavy, for those, on their own.

Aeroplanes, coaches, how they have crashed,
Vandals at large, our homes are smashed.
Our children take drugs, they sniff up glue,
They have no work, nothing to do.
Will there be a future for me, for you?
My heart is heavy, but I do not cry.

Joan Scher

From The Abandoned

The tears course down the pallid cheek;
Salt water streams whose muteness speaks.
Tense fingers grip the wooden pew,
Tense mind denies that this is you
In slender hull of oak so sleek.

Is this the vengeance deaf gods wreak?
The present grim; the future bleak?
The sudden lunge, the furtive coup;
The tears course down.

A lifelong game of hide-and-seek
Now love wells up, desires to shriek,
To cross divides of death; hack through
The awkward hours where most things true
Lay hidden, silent, shy and meek.
The tears course down.

Emma Walkers

PURE GOLD

I see the gold upon the hill,
It lights the grass with fleeting will,
I see the gold upon the shore,
On tangles, washed by waves that roar;
I seem transfixed, and I stand still.

I see the gold up in the sky,
On feathers, as a bird glides by;
I see the gold within the tree,
I see the gold.

Not the gold from underground,
Where miners dig, no light abounds;
But the golden light of the autumn sun,
Pure gold, and free for everyone.
Don't strive for gold, just look around.
I see the gold.

Barbara Henry

LISTEN - THE WIND

Listen - the wind. I hear it cry
As branches thrash against the sky,
Twigs crack in the icy sleet
And hurtle down around my feet,
While howling echoes shriek and die.
Black crows are seized, are forced to fly
On straining pinions, flung up high;
Now the chaos is complete.
Listen - the wind.

These are the quiet days, but I
Cannot rest, I wonder why
I listen in the silent heat
Of summer evenings calm and sweet,
To hear the silence still reply,
Listen - the wind.

Eve Webber

RESCUE DOG

I cannot tell my former name
So last week, 'Gemma', I became.
My master lavished time and zeal
In training me to walk to heel,
Then dumped me, - to his shame.

So, from a Rescue Home I came,
My world will never be the same.
Such horrid things I know and feel
I cannot tell.

And now I'm deaf and slightly lame
For which my former home's to blame.
My present place has great appeal,
The comfort, care and tasty meal.
Should I be asked to stay, - though game.
I cannot tell.

Bee Kenchington

Magic Moments

Magic moment! A child conceived,
sweet legacy by love bequeathed.
When would-be grannies stitched with joy
that tiny garment, cuddly toy,
too delicate to be believed.

Nine months later bright hope achieved
fulfilment, as a low voice breathed
'You have a lovely little boy'
Magic moment!

With unrelenting pain relieved,
the body's sovereignty retrieved,
wise Nature hastened to deploy
a love that nothing could destroy,
as outstretched arms her gift received.
Magic moment!

Sylvia R Reader

All My Heart

With all my heart I love Thee, Lord,
and know that I cannot afford
to waste a single hour or day
to spread the Gospel on its way;
declaring Your name is adored

by all who are joined by the cord
and seek Your face, turned heavenward.
For those in darkness, Lord, I pray
with all my heart.

And now, like Jesus, on toward
the lost and lonely; things I've stored
inside me, waiting for the day
You'll lead me to someone, to say
words long waiting to be outpoured,
with all my heart.

Hilary Philips

I Try To Control

I try to control the independent cat,
I'm wary of the fast-running rat,
Give a shiver when I meet
The mouse some find so sweet,
Warming itself on the fireside mat.

The dog I pat,
Stroke as it's sat,
With its restless feet,
I try to control.

Like the old favourite hat,
Or unruly wayward brat
Creatures are objectionable or a treat,
But would life be more complete
If I was in command, of all that
I try to control.

Colin Farmer

NATURE

The hedgerows quivered in the gale,
It seemed destruction would prevail,
The trees, if anything were worse,
In that they'd no depth to disperse
The wind. Yet they were far from frail.

The clouds most thick in their detail,
Scuttled steeply o'er hill and dale
Bringing perhaps, to all a curse,
The hedgerows quivered.

The storm continues to unveil
Its strength. Trees down, a sorry tale.
The rain is slanting, so terse
As to seem entirely adverse
To man, leaving him deathly pale.
The hedgerows quivered.

Richard Saunders

I'M OLDER NOW

The fire can burn my life away.
The clock can tick till old Domesday.
The memories come in a flash.
I'm thinking of one special bash.
One year we went on holiday.

To some place nice, a little grey,
I poke the fire and dream away.
I can recall - no balderdash!
I'm older now.

Again I wake, it's still the day,
Not time for bed to hit the hay.
I turn around to hear a crash,
My cup has gone and had to smash.
I make a sigh and have to say,
I'm older now.

Angela Helen

WHEN DARKNESS FALLS

When darkness falls what's left to hear?
As optimism turns to fear
Crowding, squashing neglected brain
Ensuring life's no longer same
For what is hazy, what is clear?

I sometimes pray there will appear
A route to lead me out of here
Enabling me to hope again
When darkness falls.

Voices echoing inside ear
Confuse, for which ones are sincere,
The ones that persecute and blame
Or those that tell me I'm still sane.
Until I know please say you're near
When darkness falls.

George Stanworth

THAT DREAM

I had that dream again last night,
Was it a nightmare? No not quite,
But I was aroused full of dread,
With unexplained thoughts in my head,
So something somewhere isn't right.

I clenched my fists, my knuckles white,
And tried to overcome that plight,
But can't ignore what lies ahead,
I had that dream.

Each thought I have, I'm filled with fright,
Perhaps I do have second-sight,
Tomorrow we may all be dead,
If no one heeds what has been said,
Dare I go on this maiden flight,
I had that dream.

Peter Chaney

HE WAS MY SON

He was my son, a boy so fine.
I prayed to Thee, Lord God devine.
Don't let him die, do your healing.
With my heart I was appealing.
I begged of you, give me a sign.

Please grant my wish, do not decline.
I feared the worst, as tears saline
Spilled forth, from shock I was reeling.
He was my son.

I cherished him for he was mine.
Now gone, I will forever pine.
Numb with grief, devoid of feeling.
In your chapel I am kneeling,
Proud of the fact, although now thine
He was my son.

Karen Tyas

MY FIRST RONDEAU

I'd bought a house, it was very old,
On floors and cupboards, there was plenty of mould.
'You're foolish' said friends, 'it's not worth a dime
You'll regret its purchase, in a short time.'
I'd gone against what I was told.

The visions of what I could do, were bold.
I'd bring in men, who'd help not scold
Soon I'll have everything looking fine.
I'd bought a house.

The men worked hard in damp and cold.
'Twas soon a spectacle to behold
Windows with a brilliant shine,
Now I could boast that it was mine
And worth its weight in gold.
I'd bought a house.

Peggy Johnson

BELL ECHOES

Bell echoes down the rolling years
extolling laughter tolling tears.
Some stones lie velveted in moss
as others roll the tempests' toss
brandishing courage scorning fears.

Life is an overcoat one wears
as shaggy sheep or wintry bears
sheltering in the skin from loss.
Bell echoes down

the time that hindsight blindly clears:
some overpaid and some arrears -
who counts the gain and who the loss,
who was the minion, who the boss -
lover and loser overhears
Bell echoes.

Shirley Beckett

LIFE'S GARDEN

The steps lead on to garden pond
Fringed with tall iris, and beyond
The garden wall the hills gleam green,
Mauve, rust or gold, a changing scene.
(Pastel today, as if crayoned.)

Safe in my nest by waving frond
Of honeysuckle, sweet and blonde
I see to where the bamboos lean
The steps lead on,

On, into life. There is no wand
To wave for ease, but, armour donned
Hard challenges embrace unseen.
Life is so rich, for each pristine.
And to this life - our common bond -
The steps lead on.

Joyce Goldie

Princess

My precious friend missed every morn
Small white dog for you no dawn
No wet black cold nose on mine
To greet me, Princess how I pine
For you, as all, were just a pawn

In life's game when you were born
To love and leave me all forlorn
As you and I were just like twine
My precious friend

You ran and jumped as high as corn
Now I feel my heart is torn
Your big brown eyes were so divine
My lasting wish is peace be thine
Why from me were you withdrawn?
My precious friend.

Elizabeth Rice

THE GHOST

She nearly died of fright last night.
The power was off, there was no light,
And groping up the stairs to bed
She met a man she knew was dead.

She said 'Good evening' to the ghost
Who glided through the newel post.
Her knees were trembling and she shook.
She simply didn't dare to look.
She nearly died.

She reached her bed and comfort found
Beneath the blankets pulled around
Her head. She couldn't breath at all,
And there was no one she could call.
So there she lay without a sound.
She nearly died.

Ann Mather

TROPICAL RAINS

I loved the rain's cascading drops,
its sparkling jewels refreshing crops,
but since that day of yesteryear
once crystal gems bring nought but fear.
As oft a deluge progress stops.

Onto African roads it plops,
driven across in bouncing hops
to swell the potholes' muddy mere.
I loved the rains.

Over the flooding ground it slops
where rich red soil no longer mops
the driven rain. No driving cheer
to wallow long in bottom gear
till flowing road the engine tops.
I loved the rains.

Jan Claxton

THIS IS THE CITY

This is the city of my birth.
Salford what's its worth!
Citizens of our real world.
Into another's name sometimes we're hurled.
We are a part, of Mother Earth.

An actual city, though not Bath.
On a hill but not a rath.
Our pride is pure, not curled.
This is the city.

True heritage, has taken our very path.
For self respect we certainly, do hath.
We're clearly seen not clouded, pearled.
Feet firmly on the ground not shaken, swirled.
Our name we'll sow, in the aftermath.
This is the city.

Harry Livesey

MY LABRADOR

My Labrador I thought I'd train
for walking her was quite a strain.
I joined up in the village hall
with other doggies large and small.
Then round the room and round again
she started sniffing a Great Dane.
Her manners really were a pain.
She quite ignored my every call,
my Labrador.

We were quite hopeless in the main.
Our confidence we could not gain.
She really does at times appal.
She wee'd and pooed in front of all.
We've not been back! I can't explain
my Labrador.

John Christopher

I Do Think On

I do think on what might there be,
Beyond the life we cannot see.
A feeling's more than a vision,
Does a criminal see beyond prison?
Little time, too much thought is the key.

I lay on the sand by the sea,
The waves washing thoughts over me.
The pebbles are hard, broken cushions.
I do think on.

My thoughts branch out like a tree,
Sleep comes in form of remedy.
My mind is sometimes on a mission,
It's the gift of acute intuition.
Before I can count up to three,
I do think on.

Julie Brace

TIME TO SLEEP

Just sleep on it, you soon will find
Your troubles you have left behind
To a bright new morn you will awake,
Your love has gone, don't cry, and shake

Or, snivel, whimper, say that life's unkind.
It's best to wait, all love is blind.
Get on with life, make up your mind
Not to tremble not to forsake
Just sleep on it.

It may take time, to be resigned
Don't sit and mope get to the grind.
Decisions you may have to take
There may be lots of plans to make.
Time to forget, that you have pined.
Just sleep on it.

A B Chabaluk

I'M TAKING IT BACK!

I'm taking it back without delay,
Lock stock and barrel as I may.
My inheritance stolen in the night,
In just a single bite,
A mauler, silky-smooth attack.

I've been ripped off
By a power-puff dragon-of.
Using his weapon of deception.
I'm taking it back!

Casting down imagination
I demand full restitution.
I moved to the land of possibility,
There I regain my integrity.
In the name of the Law of Retribution
I'm taking it back!

Verleta Malcolm

NEEDS

If all alone, then I would need
Plants and flowers to grow and seed.
And some music that's appealing
My yoga tape to keep me kneeling.
Snaps of spouse and children two indeed
And their offspring or heart would bleed.
Needles and wool for knitting, I plead
And a car to go careering.
If all alone.

No TV my thoughts to impede.
I'd scribble verse at remarkable speed.
So plenty of paper is the thing
To set my wee heart soaring
Then a happy fulfilled life I'd lead.
If all alone.

Pat Eves

THE MIRROR

The mirror shows my ageing face
deep lines of wisdom I can trace
Though folk may say I'm getting old
inside I'm young, so I am told

What's shown in front in any case
will never then take pride of place
hidden behind is me, in space
without reflection to behold
the mirror shows

The wrinkles come as in a race
with pattern made for life's embrace
the fire is hot, the passion cold
from time and tide the joys enfold.
My smiles accept the greying grace
the mirror shows.

Marian Acres

ANNE

My best friend is Anne
She is known to me . . .
As my right hand
Each time, when I do fall
She helps me to stand
Ten feet tall.

Every comfort, every need
She helps me to succeed
My thoughts, she understands
She's always there to lend a hand
Through trials and error
Anne is my mirror

Protecting my every call
Without a mention at all
No judgement does she make
My heart, she never breaks
My best friend is Anne!

Suzan Gumush

THE TIDE HAS TURNED

The tide has turned; and on the sea
A dancing light moves rhythmically,
Where merry wavelets gaily run
To meet the distant horizon.

The world grows dark. The setting sun
Inflames the sky when day is done;
The west ablaze in majesty;
The sea aglow with mystery.
The tide has turned.

The night clouds thicken; only one
Pale star has bravely shaken free
From shrouds of darkness. Men can see
Its light, which guides them safely on
To haven and blest sanctuary.
The tide has turned.

Dorothy E Richardson

UP SIGNAL HILL

Up Signal Hill the crowd ascended,
pushing and jostling no one offended,
we moved along to see the action,
full of interest whatever attraction,
On Signal Hill.

The air was filled with babbling sound,
screaming children chased around,
the atmosphere was so tremendous,
the evening sun was so stupendous,
Up Signal Hill.

The golden orb turned all to gold,
people stood and stared - both young and old,
watching as it quickly descended,
telling all the day had ended,
total silence as if arranged,
Up Signal Hill.

Mary E Cowburn

THIS GARDEN

I love this garden, small, complete,
So full of ev'rything that's sweet;
So secretly it nestles here,
And bows its tresses to the mere

Which lies beside it, within neat
And careful banks, where my small feet
Once cooled and splashed in summer heat.
My childhood's memories, so near,
Love this garden.

Now I try the rustic seat
Where, in the arbour, roses greet
My ageing senses - and my fear
My son will sell this home so dear . . .
Will other's children, running fleet,
Love this garden?

Jay

IN THE GARDEN

In the garden I'm nearer to God. I know
because after the winter winds that blow
spring comes along, warming the soil.
Soon I can start the more interesting toil,
before beginning the lawns to mow.

There's ground to be dug and seeds to sow;
from now I'm bound to be on the go.
Steaming along like a 'pot on the boil';
coming alive in the garden.

Flowers and vegetables soon will grow,
providing I treat them with all I know.
Ensuring that blight my effort won't foil;
endearing the plants as I would those Royal.
Finally, I'll have a right regal show,
for friends to see in the garden.

J A A Sharp

RADIANT MOON

Oh; radiant moon, you shine so bright,
The vast ocean lit by your wondrous light
You bathe the town and hills in gold
A sleepy town now growing old.

You shine o'er meadows lying so still
Bringing life to the stream down by the mill.
The mill long silent down the years,
Rippling stream, music to the ears
Oh; radiant moon.

Myriads of twinkling stars on high,
Through the branches a gentle sigh.
A night of wonder, filled with peace.
Magic shadows, troubles cease.
Joyful moments, winter draws nigh,
Oh; radiant moon.

Gueta Craigie

BACK HOME

Back home again is where I'll be
If fortune now should smile on me
So many times the tears I'd hide
To ease this yearning deep inside
Once more to be with family

Years ago, so foolishly
A quarrel ended bitterly
Now I've returned with swallowed pride
Back home again

I thought that nevermore I'd see
This home I've known since infancy
I knock, the door is opened wide
Rejection would be justified
But I am welcomed joyfully
Back home again.

Betty Curnow

Total Security

Did I really want total security, a spider-web site;
while the smiling cold cans and paper lawn the night?
They have achieved litter scent, made clear their way,
Now their careless present is the real today,
And can be seen, obscene by every bird in flight.

Did I really want the castle walls so tall and tight,
Turrets touching tips of tops out of sight,
The moat so impenetrably deep and ripple-sway,
Did I really want total security?

Quiet fastenings fitted to withstand all might,
Sensors carpet fastened down on every flight,
Fear to go abroad throughout night or day,
In case the invader should come, to visit or stay.
Now I find my loneliness shrouded in my sight.
Did I really want total security?

Peter Vaughan Williams

ON THE PAVEMENT

There on the pavement head on knees,
curled like autumn against the breeze,
keen indifference and stony stare
strip the branches of being bare.
Dreaming of steaming soup and cheese
flowing banquets of plenty seize
empty visions, to mock and tease
body and soul in need of care
there on the pavement.

Rapier wind cries through the trees
and raining tears fail to appease
the pain of wrongs beyond repair,
wrapping the mind with cold despair
in lonely fear, to weep and freeze
there on the pavement.

Shirley Johnson

THE PROMISE OF LOVE

Being with you is all I crave,
Hold my hands from cradle to grave.
For things we love to do together,
In sunshine or in unkind weather,
Stay with me still and do not save

When hubris strikes or some close shave,
Just anchor us in some dark cave,
I'll feel safe and would not sever,
Being with you.

Absence makes me lose my tether,
Do not fail or leave me ever,
Let no presence us deprave,
Always ever I will behave
With my very best endeavour,
Being with you.

Jean Marsden

THE TICK HAS STOPPED

The tick has stopped. It says he's gone.
The chime has sung its final song.
The dust lies thick upon the shelf
A final token of his wealth;
His epitaph: 'A Life Gone Wrong'.

Instead of where he should have shone
Home life was dull, he wanted fun.
With earnings he indulged himself.
The tick has stopped.

He left regrets, a lot undone.
His wife has no place in the sun.
Now for her dignity, herself
She struggles, old, in fragile health.
His place inside her heart is numb.
The tick has stopped.

Katherine Jane Rawlings

A Game

Life's but a game, the world's a stage:
some play with humour, some with rage
most games are cruel and so unkind
played by a power-hungry mind
Who aims to tease, throws down his gage.

Like hunted animals in a cage
we the tormentor's moods must gauge
we fence and joust, too soon we find
Life's but a game.

Role-playing calmly comes with age
'Be patient,' says the wise old sage
'Some men are ruthless, some are kind
some roads are straight, others wind and wind.'
When one Act ends we turn the page . . .
Life's but a game.

Margaret D'Sa

THE TORNADO

That wind blows cruel, increasing powers
Blind raging waves hurling showers.
Vibrant water hits the beach
Throwing boulders the shore to leech.
Foot by foot that wind devours,
Clutching, tearing the land it scours.
Strong rock before it clings and cowers
Cringing before those twists that reach.
That wind blows cruel.

Greater yet these wind-blown towers,
Spinning, writhing, for many hours.
Wind whining roar a sort of speech
Screaming out what it would us teach.
'Always greater power than ours.'
That wind blows cruel.

Elizabeth Melvin

THE MONTH OF MAY

The sky is blue, the month is May,
The song of birds is heard all day.
In gardens tulips stand up straight
And children plead to stay up late,
To catch the sun's last lingering ray.

The meadows show young lambs at play
And bluebells grace the woodland way,
As lovers pause by kissing gate.
The sky is blue.

In nearby fields the horses neigh
And swish their tails, keep flies away.
In rivers fishes nibble bait,
The sun makes everyone feel great.
On plans for leisure thoughts do stray.
The sky is blue.

Heather Middleton

I'm Glad I'm Not

I'm glad I'm not a polar bear:
I cannot stand the Arctic air,
Which is too cold for such as we;
And as for swimming in the sea,
Well, you can do so - if you dare.

But if I was a polar bear,
I'd have a thick fur coat to wear.
As furs are worn by girls, not me,
I'm glad I'm not.

Since I am not a polar bear,
With other ones my food to share -
A mate, a greedy family,
Who would not spare a crumb for me
To ease my starving - I declare
I'm glad I'm not.

Roger Williams

A Lovely Smile

A lovely smile, a freckled face.
On the outside there was no trace
of much abuse, but through the years
this child had tried to hide her fears,
Believing she was in disgrace

She had become a special case,
Now taken from the only place
She knew as home. Yet still she wears
A lovely smile

This little child now had to brace
herself, for yet another phase
in life. A foster home appears.
Mixed feelings now of joy and tears
swept over her. Still she could raise
A lovely smile.

Brenda Thorne

MEANDERING DOWN

Meandering down its beautiful course,
a tear travels so slowly, painfully forced.
A watery child, born from within sorrow,
an infanticide with no tomorrow
a product of our broken love,

a silent prayer, a liquid dove
created in the shadows of Heaven above
but sentenced to the gallows
and still a tear meanders down.

It dances, it sparkles and puts up a fight
to indignation at its brevity and plight,
addressing an anger and pain
on becoming a dried effigy a carpet stain.
A journey from the soul, from blue-fuelled sight,
and still a tear meanders down.

Mark Boardman

Urban Daydream

I yearn for peace: sun-kissed meadow,
Wild gurgling streams that freely flow,
Fells extolled in rhyme and fable,
Skiddaw, Cat Bells and Great Gable.
What beauty nature does bestow.

Each season's face our senses know.
Bleating of sheep, cawing of crow
Oust the harsh din of town's babel.
I yearn for peace.

The traffic, work pressures, cause woe.
The stress and the strain are the foe.
Free on the fells one is able
To banish the fax and the cable,
Heather or bracken as pillow.
I yearn for peace.

Shirley Richmond

AGAIN

Sad to discover again I was late
Silently silently I closed the gate
And wiping my feet on the welcome mat
I switched on the light and hung up my hat
Totally unaware of my fate
I opened the door saw the fire in the grate
A half-eaten meal on a dinner plate
And a look that said you loathsome rat
Sad to discover
Darling I love you let us not hate
I forgive you, you just couldn't wait
It's not the food or anything like that
I know you've been seeing my best friend Pat
Divorce proceedings I must instigate
Sad to discover.

F McFaul

SO LONG AGO...

So long ago, when I was young,
I knew the songs by sweet birds sung,
My heart was blithe the whole day long,
My footsteps light with strides so strong,
Head held high 'mid those I dwelt among.

With stalwart heart and healthy lung,
I climbed life's ladder, freely swung,
Nor could I think of doing wrong,
So long ago.

I did not need to hold my tongue,
Because my joy was newly sprung,
But Adam found in learning 'wrong',
That sins in Heaven don't belong,
So he was from his Eden flung,
So long ago.

Richard Styles

RONDEAU FOR THE FIRST DAY OF SPRING

Spring is here in freshest green,
The first snowdrop has been seen,
The first cuckoo has been heard,
Such an odious, un-caring bird,
Leaves take on a healthy sheen.

New petals growing in-between,
Sprouting from the bulbs unseen,
Growth that winter had deferred,
Spring is here.

Sheep are shorn to keep them clean,
Chicks peck while their mothers preen,
Lambs gambol and calves join the herd,
Something wonderful has occurred.
You must know what I mean -
Spring is here.

Andrew Fisher

Love's Rondeau

I do not ask for passion's fire
To last beyond our youth's desire
For twining limbs of summer's noon
To frolic 'neath a winter's moon.

Nor when my infant's face I see
In all its blind expectancy
Hope to find fulfilment there
For all my past and all my care -
I do not ask.

But when the future's growing short
And savour's gone from all we've bought
To find in you the answer there
For all we've seen and all we share
And wondering, find the comfort sought -
I do not ask.

Barbara Stanworth

PLIGHT OF THE FEW

The men from the Ministry wanted our village
Like a Saxon horde they could rape and pillage
Despite treetop protests and tunnels galore
The faceless throng used the weight of the law
The men from the Ministry wanted our village

Timbers cracked and the bulldozer rolled
Paradise fell and carnage unfold
And the landscape resembled a scene from the Somme
The men from the Ministry tortured our village

Half-timbered houses two centuries old
Have been moved to a site alien - cold
Where once there was laughter, freedom and light
Concrete and noise will bring its delight
As the aircraft wing in by both day and night
The men from the Ministry have taken our village.

M C Davies

Fishermen

Remember please the fishermen;
who steam to sea then back again.
They risk each trip their lives, then turn
a catch to cash and like all spurn
the snooping taxman's pen.

No suited office life for them,
their world exists 'tween keel and stem
and netting towed astern,
Remember please the fishermen.

Perhaps they prick your conscience when
your office eyes perceive but then
condemn a hard day's work's return
of honest cash, so honest earned,
That dirty workers' requiem,
Remember please the fishermen.

Eric McClurry

THOSE CHILDHOOD DREAMS

Those childhood dreams in my mind's eye
Flown away on a soundless sigh.
They say for no man time will wait
I understand now all too late
And to my youth I say goodbye.

My skies once blue now seem so grey
And stars no longer light my way;
Now all I want is to take back
Those childhood dreams.

Why do my visions never last?
Is destiny the die that's cast?
Mem'ries fall through a timeless haze,
Lingers fondly on bygone days.
What happened to the days that passed
Those childhood dreams.

Sylvia Crocker

I'M ALONE

I'm alone, once more, to face the night.
Needing, my lover of the light.
'O supreme being, home in, and see
my desperate plight - my agony.
Come closer, and erase this ache.
Please do this, Lord, for my sake!
Stay with me, until I wake,
for I couldn't bear, the reality.
I'm alone, once more.

Rock me gently, Lord, tonight,
as your look of love, burns bright.
Be a healing balm, to my troubled soul;
So tend me, now, and make me whole,
Grant me strength, when I face the fact.
I'm alone, once more.'

Patricia-Mary Gross

OUGHT FOR A LAFF

'Ought for a laff' was what he said!
A constant thought within his head.
'That's what he's like! That sort of bloke
Who's always 'on' to play a joke!'

And so it proved, that fateful day.
The last - before he passed away.
As, yet again, he played a wheeze.
His poor old wife once more he'd tease.
'Ought for a laff!'

His plan was just pretend to hang.
'She'll faint with shock! Oh, what a prang!'
Alas, the stool slipped from his feet.
The rope drew taut - the knot, so neat,
It broke his neck. Choked out the slang -
'Ought for a laff!'

J H Watson

I Close My Eyes

I close my eyes so I can't see
The signs that death is courting me.
And yet my hands still touch and stray,
Over the skin where the lumps lay.
I cry to God to hear my plea,

To heal my flesh and set me free!
In fear I fall upon my knee.
Why do I find it hard to pray?
I close my eyes.

The doctor, skilled in surgery,
Suggests a full mastectomy,
To be performed without delay,
I want to scream, yet come what may,
I'll fight and win longevity!
I close my eyes.

Jo Spencer

THIS WAS 1997

This was 1997 a year that wasn't ours, I should say,
it was as if for a crime we were being made to pay,
a debt for nothing, but misery and tears,
not a month went by, without despair or fears,

For good luck, hope and happiness, so hard we'd pray,
not what life was throwing at us, in such a cruel way,
sometimes it became so hard, to face another day,
like a dark cloud looming over us that never clears,
This was 1997.

Accidents, misfortune, the loss of a child, dismay,
we experienced events, that forever in our hearts, will stay,
people said, 'Don't worry all's not as bad as it appears,'
they weren't cursed like us, in this most terrible of years,
destiny cast bitter blows, maybe the devil came to play,
This was 1997.

Petina Anderson

HE'S BETTER OFF

He's better off, I heard her say
The one that had him put away
He couldn't cope too well at night
But otherwise, he seemed alright
He cried, but still they had their way

They took his little pal that day
Off to a dog's home far away
He was too frail to stand and fight
He's better off

The funeral was yesterday
She came to watch, respects to pay
If she's left him alone he might
Have struggled on, as was his right
She'll get her just rewards one day
He's better off?

Barbara Knight

OLDER AND WISER

When one is young and life carefree,
You think you know how love will be.
When naiveté belies one's years,
You nurture those same hopes; few fears
Can shake your sentimental tree.

So, when the truth was thrust on me,
I deepened my perplexity
By brooding on how love appears
When one is young . .

And now, I struggle to agree
That simple domesticity
Each to the other's heart endears;
For long years shared still end in tears.
But love is disinclined to see:
When one is young.

Terry Edwards

OLD TRUANT BOYS' REUNION

Gathered now in cobwebs, clutching tight the stool,
reminisce within the gloom, years of cuckoo rule,
chuckle at the memories, distant now the pain,
teachers long-gone perished, experts with a cane,
empty classes just remain, the haunted lonely fool.

Now autumn time exists, spattering rain is cool,
truant boys now captured, within life's swirling pool,
now easy are remembered, early days' swift game,
gathered now in cobwebs.

So here we go, that same ole' spool,
to slang an' tease, the long-gone ghoul,
who used to preach, life was a stain,
without his wisdom, nowt worth a gain,
'tis just a race, like wolves in wool,
gathered now in cobwebs.

Ian MacLaren

SEARCHING

I sit here searching my mind for a rhyme
I'd sit here all night but I haven't the time
No theme can I think of though I try real hard
Was it like this I wonder for all of the bards?
In need of inspiration I am awaiting a sign

Could poetry be a birthright not there to find
I know in my heart success will be mine
I must think harder though it may leave me scarred
Still I sit here searching

I must complete this stanza and do it by nine
Only three more lines and things will be fine
Are my attempts too risqué too avant-garde?
Will I receive encouragement or will I be barred?
Can't finish what I've started I'm losing my mind
And so I sit here searching.

C J Collins-Reed

ODE TO A TIGER

He remains quiet as any lamb.
For he can hunt no more to get you out of a jam.
That tiger whose younger days are o'er.
But he does not find his life a bore,
He recalls adventures, he had in days of yore.

He has now given up the game,
But he'd enjoyed his life, all the same.
However now as he nears the end,
He remains quiet.

No longer does he quietly roam,
For hungry children way back home.
Now the young have left his den,
They are all grown-up maids and men,
And as he ceases to hunt so little,
He remains quiet.

Betty Green

Almost Winter

In this grave hour of setting free
Life's embers from captivity,
Sad autumn, with her burnt-out ends,
Still lingers where the river bends,
And winter's chill yet bows the knee.

The evening's sunlit ecstasy
Awakes the dormant memory,
Whose joys October's gloom transcends
In this grave hour.

In umber stillness I would be,
Where autumn's dark conspiracy
With death in bonfire smoke ascends
Like long-forgotten dreams, and wends
The high-road to eternity
In this grave hour.

S H Smith

I Am Not Young

I am not young; I am not old,
'You're equidistant' so I'm told.
The wrinkles started just last week;
In winter when my kneecaps creak,
I blame the weather - it's the cold.

All wealth and riches - pots of gold,
Can't save me from this age I hold.
The future - can it be so bleak?
I am not young.

My story if it's ever told,
Will confess my peculiar mould.
Some say that I can be so meek,
Then divulge my tempestuous streak,
And many secrets would unfold,
I am not young.

Katrina M Greenhalf

THEY'LL NEVER KNOW

They'll never know her, when gossip is rife,
How she enters another day in her life.
A fearful heart, a soul in pain,
As each day ends, she ends the same
So many tears for all the strife,

Living the blues, cutting thought with a knife,
While they gain control of her double life.
A rag doll, whom they gave a name
They'll never know.

How long can she survive on pride,
What happens when she can no longer hide
The torment, the hurt, how can she refrain?
When peace and calm never remain.
The scars she hides, lie deep inside.
They'll never know.

Christine Nicholson

THEODORE

Without harm, he walked the seven-gated lane
daily; heedless of sea fret or chill rain
or well-whetted tongues, his mind ingrowing
and nurtured by his coming and going
treading the same paths again and again.

Churchyard mound, pit and pew were his refrain,
The cramped lives behind the cracked window-pane.
Kindly, his words belied his bestowing,
Without harm, he.

Housed under the hill, his life was plain
Only his fears wove an intricate skein.
Death's thread was scarlet, his constant knowing,
with disillusionment's bitter showing.
Hedge-priest of poverty he must remain
without.

Judith Stinton

SAILING

Upon the water I float free
And slip the ropes which tether me,
To all the woes that tire and wear
And sometimes get too much to bear,
As furious come anxieties

Then I get tired and need to be
On river or an open sea,
To rest my mind away from care
Upon the water.

Refreshed and rested I'll then be
Renewed as nature's sights I see,
I'll trim my sails for skies set fair
Where seagulls fly and watch me there,
And share their freedom time with me
Upon the water.

Barbara Pearton

OF LOVE

The art of love is hard to learn,
Each time I try it's not my turn.
Poetic words for my sweetheart,
Halfway through she'll turn and depart.
To learn the art my soul does yearn.

She'll ask me: 'How much do you earn?'
Then she tells me her cakes will burn,
Off she trots, the little upstart.
The art of love.

I try again with great concern.
What am I: a funeral urn;
No care for words that I impart,
She'll turn and run, the silly tart.
The art of love is hard to learn.
The art of love.

Paul Corrigan

FINE WINES

When I was younger, I thought of this date,
But reckoned with ageing, I'd degenerate,
How could I enjoy the millennium year?
I'm now over forty, middle-age is here,
Now it gets nearer and quickens the rate,

I'm enjoying my life, whatever my fate -
Champagne is on ice - yes celebrate,
I'll sing and I'll dance, not shedding a tear,
I was younger.

But youth wasn't all, not always so great,
Everything seemed to exaggerate,
Now it seems directions are clear,
People, not items, become much more dear,
Time has removed all the anger and hate,
I was younger.

Pat Derbyshire

When You Want Me

When you want me I will be there,
worries to burden, troubles to share,
I'll be a shoulder to cry on, arms to hold you,
I'll be with you when only a voice won't do,

when you need company, I'll be round to care,
one alone's not much fun, it's better to pair.
You can tell me anything, I'm not easy to scare,
I'm your friend, stuck on you like glue
when you want me.

Your mind, your body and soul you can bare,
how far will it go - how far do you dare?
All friends are important and this is so true,
but the most special of all to me, is you.
I love you, need you, want you? Oh yeah!
When you want me.

DJ King

A Way Out Fishy Tale

We'd waded out from water's edge
and right out to the rocky ledge,
then dipped our nets in murky holes
and poked about with oily poles
until we struck the seaweed hedge
all jellied swirling round the sedge,
then groping deep we scooped a wedge
of shingle grit from off our soles
we'd waded out.

Still further out a rusty kedge
all gnarled we found and made a pledge:
the first to catch sight of the shoals
would have to drag the loaded bowls,
piled high with fish, back on the sledge
we'd waded out.

Rosemary Keith

I Fall Asleep

I fall asleep at any time.
Is that such an horrendous crime
Just to rest a tired, weary mind?
Tired from the strain to have to find
The words to make a Rondeau rhyme.

The workshop we know ignores the grime
As sweat pools into sticky slime.
To save my eyes from going blind
I fall asleep.

Wake to the thought, when in my prime
words would flow softly and sublime
Where now it's such an awful grind
Today I often feel inclined
To use the modern way and mime.
I all asleep.

John Aldred

JUST FISHING

It's fun to fish - and popular,
Collecting minnows in a jar.
Down the canal, along its bed,
I trawl my net (or hook on thread)
With methods quite irregular.

With moustache most spectacular,
A man puffed at a huge cigar,
Watching. Although my face flushed red -
    it's fun to fish.

'How do you know where minnows are?'
(He coughed and scratched his jugular).
'How do you catch them - with stale bread?'
He asked. So I perversely said,
'The bait I use, is caviar -
    it's fun to fish.'

Pauline Pullan

THE TWO HAPPY ONES

'Twas on the brink of death we
Leapt into a world to flee
The fate so cruel to those
That wait in fear they froze:
They 'scaped the final certainty

That all foresee
In them so desperately
'Fore all life goes.
So happy now.

Boldly they swam and 'cross the lea
From their dark world to see
The liberty man knows
And can to humble pigs propose
From out their shuttered agony.
So happy now.

John Amsden

SPRING TREADS SOFTLY

Spring treads softly, doesn't dither,
Clears the ice floes from the river,
Gently calls the birds to sing,
To building nests their mates to bring,
With trilling notes to quiver.

Winter's still close, and we shiver,
March winds dancing here and thither,
Maybe winter still reigns king,
Spring treads softly.

Wild flowers growing now come hither,
Green shoots, catkins growing chipper,
New-born creatures, nature's caring,
Quietly does the Welkin ring,
Dulcet notes of flute and zither,
Spring treads softly.

Ivy Allpress

NO RECIPE

It's not easy to find time each day
Why is it so hard to pray?
Perhaps I really try too hard
I read words from a Prayer Card
I wish there was another way!

To just talk to God . . . that is to pray,
Can I tell Him what I've done today?
But I hold Him in such high regard
It's not easy.

He taught us special words to say
The Lord's Prayer is still the same today.
Or take words from our own Scot's Bard.
Holy Willie's Prayer is not too hard.
It's not easy.

Mary Anne Scott

OUR POOR EARTH

Our poor Earth suffers so,
Now the last wild forests go.
Polar ice-caps weep with heat
- Global warming is at the seat
Of our problems, don't you know;

Hot the burning forests glow,
While folk say you should show
Some small mercy as you beat
Our poor Earth.

Now the gathering storms blow
And the swollen rivers flow
- Still the politicians bleat,
Doing nothing as they meet,
Allowing greed to lay low
Our poor Earth.

J D Bailey

I Give Up

Oh woe is me, alas alack
For I am nothing but a hack
No inspiration seethes in me
I lack the verve of poesy
Although my feeble brain I rack
I always seem to go off track
Before I get it down in black
And white; results are as you see
Oh woe is me.

I've no excuse for being slack
It seems I just don't have the knack,
I'm sure I'll never earn a fee
So I'll just sit here by the sea
And listen to my knuckles crack.
Oh woe is me.

J C Fearnley

Think Of The Words

Think of the words for a song
write them however long
even if it is wrong
sing it as you go along
see how you get along

Writing musical notes may take long
when completed you have a song
to be a very good song
think of the words

Now that you have written a song
time it and see how long
check if grammatically wrong
your message must be strong
sing it in front of a throng
think of the words

Albert Moses

TRUST ME HE SAID

Trust me he said this is not place for you to stay.
Sorry you flew through my window today
Steady your wings and you will see
I will do all I can to set you free
So he whistled a tune and thought of a way.

He saw by her feathers she was trembling and sad.
What could he do to make her glad?
Then he reached for a soft cloth to cover the bird.
Trust me he said.

Gentle hands then took her to the open window above
as the bird felt the air she became calm like a dove.
With the uplift of her wings she was ready to fly
all gone was her fear as she soared up in the sky.
In her ears as she flew, the words echoed in love.
Trust me he said.

Hazel Wilson

I Never Learn

I never learn. I twist and turn,
skip and dance to achieve the burn,
bump and grind to pulsating sound
to shed excess of Christmas round.
A sylph like figure now I yearn.

I stretch and strain, my regime stern
to get my figure to return
to what it was, not over round.
I never learn.

My figures caused my mate concern
as now it's shaped more like an urn
no hourglass figure to be found,
so pounding streets I will be bound.
Perhaps next year the food I'll spurn.
I never learn.

Peter Madle

GRANNIE'S LITTLE ANGELS

Grannie's little angels, lent from 'up on high'
Hush my own wee darlings! I'll sing a lullaby!
Daniel and Connor my tiny Grandsons
How much does Grannie love you? Tons 'n' tons 'n' tons!

One is a red-head, the other a blonde
Loving to feed ducks down at the pond!
See-saws 'n' swings? Of them they are fond!
So full of life - they make me feel young
Grannie's little angels!

Two pairs of mischievous deep blue eyes!
Trouble looking where to happen! Two big sighs!
They toddle to me - we have such fun!
Two little Grandsons both aged one!
You've made my life so complete!
Grannie's little angels!

Patricia Cairns Laird

OUT OF THE DARKNESS

Come what may, for sure it matters not
I'll take that cast from fate's mixed pot
The dregs of life once mine to trace
Have since left me, quit in sore disgrace
As here I rise from dung heap's rot

My spirit soars to seek a destined slot
From a cowed past, now long since forgot
To fly far away above the common place
Come what may

Where larks and swallows flit, swoop and swot
Great joy and new elation has me trot
Nor care I as in my driven haste
Emotions bared and all fast laid to waste
I will wallow in my new-found lot
Come what may

Sheila Scott

MILLENNIUM RONDEAU

So now - farewell old century,
Your days and months and years must be
Soon chronicled on history's page
Committed to a bygone age . . .
A slowly fading memory.

A new millennium we see
Approach with high expectancy
Upon our frail and human stage
So now - farewell.

And looking t'ward eternity
What does the future now foresee?
Will nations still with hatred rage?
Upon mankind vile warfare wage?
Two thousand troubled years will flee
So now - farewell.

Kath Hurley

GLASS SHARDS SHATTERED AND SPLINTERED

Glass shards, shattered and splintered distort and reflect
Life's joy and despair with confusing effect:
Image of chaos, of both brilliance and pain,
Dazzling the vision, puzzling the brain,
Eternal conundrum to leave us perplexed.

We step close to see them and then we are checked
By a lack of courage, our abiding defect,
Staring, retreating till they are just plain
Glass shards, shattered and splintered.

The lesson is clear and is: 'Only connect'.
And what is before us is our defect:
For we cannot achieve the ultimate gain
Until we accomplish and also retain
A view of our life that does not reflect
Glass shards, shattered and splintered.

Kathrine Talbot

SOAPS

I'm hooked on 'Soaps' I will admit.
This nightly treat I won't omit.
The burning question to decide -
Will Barry Grant still rule *Brookside*?

EastEnders battle - never quit,
Though now and then they do a flit,
Back in the pub they're fighting fit.
The villains will not be denied,
I'm hooked on 'Soaps'.

With me *The Street*'s the biggest hit,
Deidre's angst, Maud's acerbic wit -
Adversity must be defied
By women in whom hope has died.
Their dedication shows true grit,
I'm hooked on 'Soaps'.

M E Lavin

Now

Ponder this, my good friend,
what is life, when will it end.
Not requested, no choice involved,
no guarantee, that you'll get old.
No clue, what's round the bend.

No time to waste, none to lend,
focus your life, and amend.
Mistakes, can be absolved.
The time is now.

What has passed, is not a trend,
you have a choice, ways to mend.
Power to you, has been devolved,
use it till, new ways resolved.
Then a new message send.
The time is now.

Jack Greaves

WINTER'S GIFT

Grey fingers snatch my breath away,
Frost's sparkle heralds winter's day,
Snow's diamond crystals silent drift
Its soft white blanket cover swift
To clothe old autumn's sad display.

Cold sun illuminates my way,
Chill winter's moon silvers the play
Of snowflakes, as in breeze they lift
I long for spring.

Ice hugs the waiting buds of May,
Festoons of icicles array
Each glistening roof, each snow-filled rift,
Its necklace Mother Nature's gift
Of beauty. Bone-chilled yet I pray
I long for spring.

Gwen Stone

No More Goodbyes!

'No more goodbyes!' You waved your hand -
I didn't really understand
That when you walked out through the door
I wouldn't see you any more.
You went off to a hostile land,

And all the things that we had planned,
The dreams, the hopes - all built on sand,
We couldn't guess what lay in store -
No more goodbyes!

We kissed so hard, I hugged you, and
'Please come back soon' was my command.
You died in someone else's war
Upon a far off foreign shore.
Bereft and desolate I stand -
No more goodbyes!

Eleanor Rogers

STRANGER

I am just a stranger today,
I sadly thought making my way
from the fine rail station to town
not wanting to be on my own.
It was a place I loved to stay.

She used to meet me, now I'll pay
for all that joy gone far away.
This road many times I've been down
but now I am just a stranger.

York Minster is the place to pray
but all my dreams have turned to clay.
I sat in the York Arms with a frown,
where were the friends I'd once known?
We used to have so much to say.
I am just a stranger.

Guy Fletcher

LOVE IS CARING

Love is caring, love is kind
Love is sharing, love is blind
love is all things great and small
Love is there to answer the call
To feel for others as they feel for you
Never reject a love that grew
For love is for all not the few
Do not conceal how you feel for
Love is caring

What is life without love
Given at birth from above
To enjoy with happiness and peace
And in your growth will increase
To ease the heart from pain for
Love is caring

W Beavill

Follow The Sun

Follow the sun watch it rising
Long damp shadows slowly dying
Blow on the glass, feel the heat burn
Listen to your heart beat, don't turn
Away for the sun is shining.

Forget dark skies, winter sighing
Cold sad days, the ivy climbing
Soft light lingers, it's now I yearn
To follow the sun.

Leave far behind days of striving
Touch hot sand the salt wind driving
Spray stings my cheeks the rough seas churn
I lie asleep, how the sun burns.
In my dreams I keep on trying
To follow the sun.

Jan Ingram McCaffery

TIME STANDS STILL

Now time stands still as I sit and think
Deep in thought I start to sink
I drift into sleep and now I doze
Bright my dreams, colours, prose.
Surrounds and cushions, soft as mink.
While quiet thoughts begin to link,
Deep from my imagination drink
And poetry from it flows
Now time stands still.

Back I come from the abyss brink
But still I sit quiet and think
About the theme that my mind chose
Another poem is born and grows
I write it down with pen and ink
Now time stands still.

Anne Jones

I Will Try Again

I will try again, with head held high
to mend the orb that dares to fly
without myself on board at all,
feeling free as it hears the call.
Sadly I watch and give a sigh

as in the air it goes awry.
It must come back on earth to lie.
I wait until it starts to trawl;
I will try again.

It cost a lot of money to buy.
Everyone said that I was the guy
that had the most ambitious gall.
But the higher you fly the further you fall.
So, if it lands somewhere that's dry,
I will try again.

Mildred Mayes

I Love My Garden

I love my garden, it's my favourite place
Looking out of the window I fondly gaze
At what I've created, the work's all my own
The path and the terrace are laid in stone.
The rose beds, cut in, each other face
Buds nodding their heads in perpetual grace.
I sit on the bench nearby where I find solace
And peace in the twilight hour, all alone.
I love my garden.

It took many years of toil to fill the space
With shrubs and trees, colourful plants to set it ablaze.
Each year new species of flora I've sown
And watched with interest how they have grown.
There's lots more to do, but though I've slowed my pace
I love my garden.

Lisa Wolfe

I Shall Not Cry

I shall not cry though my heart aches
For the hard pathway in life some people have to take
When I see the image of a child, on the television screen
Foraging for food, his body small and lean
As the sun beats down, and his ebony body bakes.

Either in the streets or by the dried-up lakes
As with a rumbling stomach, at dawn he wakes
To face another day in this life that's cruel and mean
I shall not cry.

Up he gets, and from his clothes the dust he shakes
But what difference to life a little help makes
Aid will mean that onto nourishing food he can wean
With shelter he can keep himself protected and clean
With help he can get a few lucky breaks
I shall not cry.

Margaret Winrow

Do Eat These Nuts

Do eat these nuts you birds, don't fight
Remember manners, be polite,
My tranquil garden where at ease
You nest and chatter in my trees

Brings me great joy and such delight
When bathed in sun and summer's light
From dappled trunk, to leafy height;
Feel free to peck them as you please,
Do eat these nuts.

A kestrel hovers like a kite
My birds, they've gone, all taken flight
No feathered bundles left to seize
Just naked leaves to tempt the breeze
Which springs this shadow like a sprite.
Do eat these nuts.

Nicholas Winn

FLIP

Credit discredit. Like some board game
battered in a long-stay ward,
but it's played everywhere. The game
flicks pain to good and good to blame
or power or weakness or reward.

Both sides of this game's cards record
the moves, but how each player's scored
turns on which side lands up, which name,
credit discredit.

Fine honesty or mere discord,
beauty or waste, faith's risks or fraud,
thankless unstinting as you claim
or blackmail, discipline or maim:
:
make up the rules, play them when bored,
credit discredit.

Aidan Baker

BATHED IN THE MOONLIGHT

Bathed in moonlight, a summer's night.
A wood of silver - shining bright
And on each twig, and bough, and tree,
Secrets were then revealed to me -
There in the moonbeam's shining light.

Exposed for my extreme delight,
Windflowers shone. A virgin white
And foxes playing I could see -
Bathed in moonlight.

Beyond the wood in frozen plight,
A rabbit watched in spellbound fright,
And wondered what it's fate might be
With terror in extremity -
Scared! Then to flee in hopeless flight -
Bathed in moonlight.

Jack Judd

EVACUATION

A steam train at the station, screeching to a halt.
Children staring wide-eyed, parents in revolt -
Weeping for their children taken from their arms
Away to distant places to villages and farms
To strangers, and emotional assault.

A whistle blows a vacant sound
Tears flowing freely to the ground
The dread of facing the unknown
And the blind hate.

The chug, chug, chug . . . a puff of smoke
Taking from the bitter folk
Their lives of love and happiness
So taken for granted . . . now a mess
People crying fit to choke
With blind hate.

Doreen Welby

Hold On

Trying to hold on, with all my might
to that which is dearest in my sight
I will always love the way
you are with me, each passing day.

This to me, through endless night
forever more, a love torn plight
to be with you, come what may
I will try to hold on

to my love for you, hold you tight
forever more I face the fight
to have you here, never go away,
to keep your love, is all I pray.
While you are to me a guiding light
I will try to hold on . . .

To you.

Pamela Girdlestone

INFORMATION

We hope you have enjoyed reading this book - and that you will continue to enjoy it in the coming years.

If you like reading and writing poetry drop us a line, or give us a call, and we'll send you a free information pack.

Write to :-
**Poetry Now Information
1-2 Wainman Road
Woodston
Peterborough
PE2 7BU
(01733) 230746**